Original title:
Discovering the Meaning of Life Through Doodles

Copyright © 2025 Creative Arts Management OÜ
All rights reserved.

Author: Lila Davenport
ISBN HARDBACK: 978-1-80566-115-3
ISBN PAPERBACK: 978-1-80566-410-9

The Simple Complexity of a Drawing

A circle here, a squiggle there,
In my chaos, I find flair.
The lines, they twist and loop in glee,
My masterpiece, a sight to see.

A cat with wings, a fish on a tree,
Such wondrous sights all next to me.
With every stroke, the laughter grows,
Who knew a doodle had such prose?

A thought escapes, it spirals wide,
Through scribbles made, my joys abide.
A crooked smile, a frown so bright,
In simple forms, I find delight.

With crayons bright and pens in hand,
I travel to a doodle land.
In every mark, a tale unfolds,
The art of life in scribbles told.

Colors that Speak of Being.

Crimson laughs, a violet sigh,
Yellow sunbeams in the sky.
Each color whispers sweet and bold,
A rainbow's tale laughingly told.

With blobs and dots, giggles arise,
My palette dances; oh, what a surprise!
Each hue a quirk, each shade a jest,
In playful strokes, I find my rest.

Blue like the ocean, green like the grass,
In painted dreams, time seems to pass.
Mixing laughter with every hue,
The colors speak, they sing what's true.

A splash of teal, a pop of pink,
In bright delight, I pause to think.
As crayons chatter, my heart takes wing,
In every scribble, joy's what they bring.

Whispers in Pen Strokes

With every stroke, a whisper flows,
A secret shared where laughter grows.
An owl wears shoes, a frog wears a crown,
Such silly tales can turn a frown.

In gentle arcs and swirls so small,
Funny figures bound and fall.
A doodle dance, a paper flight,
The world awakes with pure delight.

Silly smirks and goofy grins,
My pen, it scribbles, my heart just spins.
The unexpected in every line,
Brings out the joy, like sparkling wine.

To draw is to dive in a sea of grace,
Where life's absurdities find a place.
In strokes that mix the trivial and deep,
Funny whispers are ours to keep.

Inkwell Journeys

In an inkwell deep, my thoughts take sail,
A paper boat on a whimsical trail.
With cap off, I pour out my dreams,
In magical realms, nothing's as it seems.

Each puddle of ink, a world to explore,
A place for giggles and so much more.
With quirk-filled creatures to meet and greet,
Life's silly puzzles beneath my seat.

A hedgehog in socks, a dog dressed in stripes,
In my doodle land, nothing stereotypes.
Graphs of laughter, charts of glee,
Every ink splash adds to my spree.

So grab a quill, let's join the ride,
On a journey where joy and laughter abide.
In every swirl and jolly design,
You'll find a piece of the absurd divine.

Stories in Silhouette

With a pencil gripped tight in hand,
I sketch a cat that takes a stand.
It dances wildly, leaps around,
In doodles strange, my joy is found.

A tree with legs, it runs so fast,
In my imagination, it's unsurpassed.
A bird in sunglasses, cool and bright,
Waves at the sun with sheer delight.

A fish on land, a toe with shoes,
My art's a party, it never snooze.
Each line I draw, it's pure and free,
My laughter spills in lines of glee.

Through whimsy, I unlock the door,
To worlds where odd is never a bore.
In silhouette, my heart takes flight,
Each doodle casts a grin so bright.

The Meaning Behind the Marks

A squiggly line that turns to a worm,
With every stroke, new wonders affirm.
This doodle moon, so big and round,
Is where my dreams can oft be found.

A hat upon a fish's head,
In a world where socks are never wed.
Crayons clash in bright, bold hues,
My paper army of silly views.

A snowman's hat and a rocket shoe,
In every mark, a laugh shines through.
My art's a riddle, quirky and sly,
As I let my fancies fly high.

Beneath my hand, the magic sparks,
With every scribble, joy embarks.
Tracing laughter in every part,
My doodle dreams a work of heart.

Fluid Fascinations

Lines whirl and twirl like gigs in rain,
A dancing dinosaur, it's never plain.
With flecks of joy in every stroke,
I sketch a world where puns provoke.

A teapot sings with a smile so wide,
While cookies dance, they cannot hide.
Each page is splattered, colors blend,
A doodled party that never ends.

Look! A mouse wearing a tiny hat,
Sees a cat and dances—imagine that!
The twist of nought—it's all a game,
Doodles laughing, never shame.

In fluid strokes, I find my glee,
With every doodle, I just decree.
Life's a canvas, bright and wide,
With silly creatures that abide.

Scribbles of Serenity

A wobbly heart drips down the page,
A fish with glasses, quite the sage.
With every curve, the giggles sprout,
In doodle-land, no one's left out.

A square cloud floats in a lemonade sky,
While pickle people just stroll by.
My fingertips dance in candy hues,
Each scribble sings with joyful news.

Worms with hats on a rollercoaster,
Twist and swirl, I doodle faster!
In each silly twist, a jest or cheer,
Scribbles summon a playful sphere.

In serene chaos, I find the thrill,
Each line and curl gives me a chill.
Everyone smiles, it's clear to see,
My doodled world is where I'm free.

Curved Paths of Contemplation

A scribble here, a squiggle there,
Thoughts bouncing like a rubber band.
Each curve reveals a hidden flare,
As laughter meets a doodle's hand.

In margins of my busy notes,
A silly monster starts to play.
With lemon hats and jelly boats,
Life's conundrums fade away.

A smile emerges in each line,
Pickles dancing, cats on skates.
Through wild sketches, I define,
The quirky charms my soul creates.

A splash of ink, a wink of fate,
My doodles whisper, "Don't you fret!"
For in these curves, I captivate,
A playful path I won't regret.

The Colorful Quest Within

In a box of crayons, bold and bright,
I set sail on my rainbow quest.
Unicorns dance in pure delight,
Each color's tales, a conundrum fest.

The blue scribbles lead to outer space,
While green roads wind through candy lands.
With my trusty pencil, I embrace,
A journey drawn, where joy expands.

A red balloon flies high above,
It carries worries like a kite.
With doodles warm as a bear hug,
I find my dreams in colors light.

Each line I sketch, a hint of cheer,
With laughs and whimsy intertwined.
In every doodle, love draws near,
A vibrant heart, one twist defined.

Erasers and Epiphanies

With an eraser in my hand,
I start my canvas, blank and wide.
Mistakes transform to happy bands,
Where silly thoughts and giggles ride.

An octopus made of purple cheese,
Dropping wisdom, what a sight!
Each scribble gives my mind some ease,
In this circus of delight.

Some lines are jumbled, some are neat,
But every stroke helps me explore.
It's better than a bland old sheet,
As thoughts arise like crafts galore.

Each blunder leads to new designs,
Erasers dance and skip around.
In doodles bright, my heart aligns,
Foundations in small quirks abound.

Patterns of the Soul's Pursuit

In patterns formed of squiggly grace,
I pen my hopes in carefree arts.
With every twist, I find my space,
As doodles bloom, my journey starts.

A cat with glasses wears a crown,
In funky hats, they teach me truth.
While silly monsters bounce around,
They share the wisdom of my youth.

A circle spirals, turning round,
Connecting dreams from here to there.
In playful sketches, I have found,
The joy of living without care.

So let the ink flow wild and free,
For in my doodles lies the key.
Each line a laugh, each stroke a spree,
Life's canvas is where we're meant to be.

Delicate Traces

On napkins, dreams do float,
With swirly lines and a cartoon goat.
A scribble here, a doodle there,
Each sketch whispers secrets to share.

Forgotten thoughts like dust at play,
Join the dance in a quirky way.
My pen becomes a laughing friend,
In every curve, my worries bend.

A stick figure sighs, needs a break,
With every doodle, new jests I make.
Life splashed on paper, a colorful spree,
As giggles tumble like leaves from a tree.

So grab your pencil, don't delay,
Let the ink spill in a wild ballet.
For every line that twirls and bounces,
Life's silly truths are what it flounces.

Sketching a New Horizon

With each stroke on this barren page,
I create a world that's all the rage.
Silly faces with big googly eyes,
As the sun smiles back from candy skies.

A flying toaster in morning light,
Spreads butter clouds, what a sight!
Each character tells a story so sweet,
Laughter bubbles at their tiny feet.

A scribble of dreams in bold hues,
With runaway thoughts, I cannot lose.
In the margins, my musings collide,
A whirlpool of fun I take in stride.

So come join this raucous parade,
Where fortunes are cast, and worries fade.
In this doodle world, wild and free,
We sketch our joy, just you and me.

The Path of a Pencil

A lonely pencil rolls away,
Doodling paths where giggle-fays.
It hops to life with a cheerful trace,
Every line draws forth a smiling face.

Wiggly worms in rainbow hues,
Twisting tales like old-time blues.
They burrow deep through pages bold,
In squiggly secrets, laughter unfolds.

A knight in capes of spaghetti bright,
Fights the dragon of a mundane night.
With every twist, my heart does race,
As absurd adventures take their place.

So wander down this quirky road,
Let doodles lighten every load.
For in these sketches, oh so small,
Life's silly magic is for us all.

Introspective Illustrations

In the quiet of my crafty nook,
A flip of paper reveals my book.
Each doodle blooms as I poke and prod,
In whimsical chaos, I nod and nod.

A dog wearing glasses, so refined,
Complains about a world unkind.
With every scribble, I find new cheer,
In the laughter, my worries disappear.

A sun that farts with every ray,
Brings giggles bright to the dullest day.
Each line a door to jest and jest,
In playful patterns, I seek my quest.

So let your pencil dance and play,
Sketch your thoughts, let fun slay.
For in these jests of simple bliss,
We fashion life with doodles of bliss.

Playful Patterns of Purpose

In margins deep, my thoughts run free,
With squiggles bold, they dance with glee.
A cat with wings? A spork on a tree,
These little doodles say, "Just be me!"

From stick-figure kings to knights in socks,
I laugh at worlds where logic mocks.
Each line a journey, each curve unlocks,
My own universe within these blocks.

With every spiral, a giggle grows,
In silly hats, my pencil flows.
I sketch the joy, as the imagination glows,
Life's absurdity in doodles shows.

So, grab your pen and draw a dream,
Where rubber ducks and jellybeans beam.
In wild creations, there's always a theme—
Life's goofy chase is always supreme!

When Colors Speak

Crayons chatter when the sun's not bright,
In technicolor whispers, they share delight.
A purple elephant, a pizza that's light,
In every hue, a giggle ignites.

The pinks and yellows hold a secret so clear,
Creating a rainbow of silly cheer.
My canvas holds more than just what appears,
A world of laughter and whimsical gears.

Splotches and splatters, a hilarious quest,
Where broccoli trees wear jackets, impressed.
In this mad land, the fun never rests,
And every bright stroke is life's little jest.

So color outside, where ideas can leap,
In palettes of joy, the memories keep.
With playful shades, my heart takes a leap,
Where laughter's the harvest, and bliss is the sweep!

Freehanded Insights

With a flick of the wrist, the magic begins,
As wiggly lines turn into silly twins.
A turtle in sneakers, while the laughter spins,
In every round shape, a giggle wins.

Not all the doodles are clever or neat,
A bizarre parade of laughs on repeat.
From crumpled pages to misplaced feet,
Life's joy can be found in this comic sheet.

Each shaky scribble unveils a bright grin,
In wobbly letters, the fun's just within.
Exploring the chaos, let the laughter in,
Every freehanded stroke, a whimsical spin.

So pen in hand, let your spirit run wild,
In a doodle-filled world, we're all just a child.
With humor as fuel, the stress is beguiled,
Through sketches and smiles, our hearts are compiled!

The Scribbled Symphony

In swirling notes of ink, a melody thrives,
A symphony of chaos in which joy derives.
With doodled instruments, the laughter arrives—
Each silly sketch of a band that survives.

A saxophone cat sings off-tune and proud,
While drumsticks parade in a jolly crowd.
The harmony's wacky, and laughter's allowed,
In a world filled with doodles, the fun's always loud.

With fingers inky and smiles so wide,
We march to a rhythm, with giggles as guide.
In every erratic line, pure joy can reside,
The world of free drawing, our colorful ride.

So dance with your pencil, let whimsy curl,
Each scribble a note in life's funny swirl.
In this vibrant orchestra, we twirl and whirl,
Finding humor in chaos, our spirits unfurl!

Ink Trails of Thought

In a world of swirls and curls,
My pen leaps, my mind unfurls.
Each scribble a moment, a quirk,
As laughter hides in my artwork.

A fish on a bike, a cat with shoes,
Each doodle brings joyful news.
What is life? Just a comic strip,
With giggles tucked in every flip.

The coffee cup wears a silly grin,
While dancing donuts swirl within.
Each line a clue, a playful tease,
In this gallery, I find my ease.

With colors bright, I take a chance,
Each sketch a silly, joyous dance.
If life's a joke, let's draw it wide,
Laughing as we take each stride.

Whispers in the Sketchbook

In my sketchbook, whispers flow,
A turtle winks, a snail says, 'Go!'
What's this tale on page so bright?
A dragon's hat? That feels just right.

With tiny stars that giggle and shine,
And stick-figure friends standing in line.
Each doodle wears a smile to share,
In the realm of ink, I find my flair.

A robot's dance, an octopus tease,
Every stroke brings me to my knees.
The paper laughs, it's full of fun,
Life's oddities, all wrapped in one.

In sketches wild, I chase the day,
With humor tucked in every sway.
Lost in doodles, I have found,
A funny world, where joy abounds.

Doodles of Destiny

With every line, I sketch my fate,
A cat in boots that won't be late.
A world so strange, so full of cheer,
My doodles tell me what I hear.

A dancing chair, a singing tree,
Life's hilarious for those who see.
The laughter spills from pencil tips,
As destiny winks and flips its scripts.

A sandwich sings a tune so bold,
While running cheese just can't be sold.
In squiggles, I find my light,
With every twist, the future's bright.

So grab a pen, take off your shoes,
Join in the fun, it's yours to choose.
A scribble here, a giggle there,
In whimsy, life's secrets lay bare.

The Untold Tales of a Pencil's Dance

My pencil jumps, it loves to play,
Drawing silliness night and day.
An alien chef with pancakes high,
Makes every meal a reason to fly.

With every stroke, a tale begins,
A rabbit in socks, a race with spins.
Life's no puzzle, just laugh and doodle,
As every curve becomes a poodle.

A slice of cake with legs to run,
In my drawings, all's meant for fun.
Sketches prance like kids on the street,
Every doodle brings joy, oh so sweet.

A pencil's dance, it sways and twirls,
In this funny life, it unfurls.
Grab your art, let giggles gleam,
In these wild scribbles, we find our dream.

The Playfulness of Perception

In every squiggle, laughter flies,
A wiggly worm in a tie, oh my!
Cupcakes with wings and shoes that grin,
What could be better than doodling in?

Think outside the box, let chaos reign,
A cat in a hat jumping on a train.
Drawn dreams dance in a wobbly line,
Each scribble's a secret, a riddle, divine.

Unraveled Thoughts in a Sketch

A fish with a mustache swims through the page,
While ants play poker, it's all the rage.
A tree wears glasses, sipping on tea,
What wisdom they share, so silly and free!

Inside the margins, wild towns exhibit,
Unraveled thoughts in a fantastical bib.
Each curve a giggle, each dot a cheer,
Who knew the mind could be this clear?

The Universe in a Doodle

Galaxies swirl in a cereal bowl,
Spaceships made from a pop can's roll.
Stars giggle down in bright yellow ink,
As scribbles of wisdom encourage us to think.

A sun with sunglasses, oh what a sight,
Waves riding cats, they dance in delight.
Conversations in loops, with laughter we share,
In the universe of doodles, there's magic in air.

Whimsical Paths to Clarity

A pencil leads us on paths quite bizarre,
Chasing a rabbit who wants to drive a car.
With every twist, we round the bend,
In doodle-land, all rules suspend.

A flying fish on a swing takes a turn,
While a chair plays chess, what will we learn?
Each line is a journey, strange and bright,
In every corner, there's joy in sight.

Figments on a Page

A scribble here, a squiggle there,
My thoughts escape without a care.
With stick figures that dance and prance,
I laugh aloud at their silly chance.

Crayons clash in a riotous hue,
As my doodles form a party crew.
They joke and wiggle, take a bow,
And I can't help but smile right now.

When I draw a cat that sings out loud,
It bumbles a tune before the crowd.
My pencil whispers secrets, mean,
Of a party with no time to glean.

In a world where lines run wild and free,
My doodles hold the key to glee.
Each stroke of ink, a burst of cheer,
Where whimsy reigns, no need to fear.

The Quiet Marks of Being

In corners of my mind, they play,
The doodles that brighten up my day.
A little frog in a tiny hat,
Chasing thoughts like a curious cat.

A lollipop tree, so fun and sweet,
Greets me with a tap-dancing beat.
It swings and sways, oh what a treat,
While my mind finds rhythm in doodled feet.

With each mark made in styles so bold,
The quiet tales of my life unfold.
A world where laughter leads the way,
In the strokes of color, my spirit plays.

These sketches breathe a giddy notion,
Filling my heart with joyful emotion.
In this silence, giggles thrive,
Like doodles that dance and come alive.

Sketches of Solitude

In my corner, I doodle away,
A fish with glasses that loves ballet.
A penguin in shorts goes for a run,
In a world where doodles have their fun.

A cloud with a face begins to joke,
Turning my worries to wispy smoke.
With every squiggle, laughter I glean,
Sketches of solitude, so serene.

A sun with a smile, bright and large,
Directs the dance, it's in charge.
While trees with arms are having a race,
And butterflies twirl in the open space.

Each funny figure spins a tale,
In a quiet world where giggles prevail.
In these sketches, joy takes its flight,
Where boredom's a ghost that's out of sight.

Ink-Stained Reflections

With ink-stained fingers, I sketch my woes,
A snail that wears a tutu with bows.
It prances on toes, oh what a sight,
Flipping my frown to a giggle delight.

Each line tells a joke as it flows with flair,
A dragon that's shy, hiding under a chair.
Reflecting on life through whimsical laughs,
In each doodle, I find silly paths.

From polka-dot clouds to a dancing chair,
The world of my doodles is filled with air.
Where shadows have fun and laughter ignites,
And seriousness takes its time for the flights.

So here's to the play in my ink-stained dreams,
Where the simplest things burst into beams.
In every sketch, a moment, a breeze,
I paint my life with doodles that please.

An Odyssey in Ink

In the margins my sketches roam,
Cats with hats and birds with foam.
Monsters dance, with wobbly legs,
Drawing smiles like sunny pegs.

Adventures penned in doodle style,
Scribbles brightening every mile.
Each line a twist, a comic spree,
Ink spills laughter, wild and free.

Moments of Mathematical Mayhem

In a classroom, numbers swirl,
Graphs go crazy, curls unfurl.
Doodles bouncing off the page,
Adding silliness to the stage.

Calculus in squiggly font,
Geometry shapes, a playful jaunt.
Equations dance, a wobbly tune,
Math might just need a cartoon.

Whirls of Enigma

Circles spin in whacky ways,
Lines get lost in a doodle maze.
With dots and squiggles, thoughts take flight,
Inky realms of pure delight.

Secrets hidden in a scribble,
Why is that cat acting so dribble?
Each wavy stroke tells a tale,
Laughing at life, we prevail.

Portraits of the Unseen

A portrait made with a playful hand,
Stick figures arguing, isn't it grand?
Eyes wide open, yet nothing's there,
Imaginary friends fill the air.

With each little sketch, they come alive,
A dragon in pajamas ready to dive.
Ink stains laugh at what we can't see,
Embracing the silly, just let it be.

Scribbled Secrets

In margins wide, my dreams run free,
A stick figure dog, just as happy as he.
With squiggles and swirls, my thoughts take flight,
Coffee spills and chaos - what a delight!

A worm in a hat, oh what a sight,
He wiggles and dances, full of delight.
A frown on his face, yet striking a pose,
Life's silly moments, each doodle does pose.

Beneath the couch, my secrets reside,
In crumpled up papers, my giggles I hide.
What's life, you ask? A doodle, my friend,
Just color it bright, let your laughter extend!

So grab those crayons, your mind to unbind,
Create your own madness, of limitless kind.
For in every sketch, a riddle may lay,
Just laugh at the mess; it's a colorful play!

Kaleidoscope of Ideas

A circle here, a line so straight,
I doodle my worries, it feels first-rate.
A cat with a hat, perchance wearing shoes,
In this whirling world, I pick and choose.

An octopus juggling, now that's pure class,
While fish play cards, they're sassy and brash.
Each swirl brings laughter, I giggle and grin,
With silly creatures, where do I begin?

In margins and corners, ideas collide,
Like confetti they scatter, cannot divide.
The world spins around in colors so bold,
As I doodle my dreams, in stories retold.

So let your pencil dance, let your laughter ring,
In a whirl of colors, the joy it will bring.
Life's a canvas bright, so playful and grand,
Each doodled delight, by your own hand!

The Palette of Possibilities

With reds and blues, my thoughts intertwine,
A chicken in slippers, oh how divine!
Each stroke of the brush, a giggle or two,
In this tiny world, there's always something new.

A lion in pajamas, snoring away,
While birds debate politics, playing all day.
A rainbow peacock on a skateboard flies,
In the chaos of colors, my spirit just sighs.

Through scribbles and splashes, I find my way,
To laugh at the nonsense, come what may.
What's life but canvas, for doodles galore?
A world of possibilities, waiting to explore!

So grab that paintbrush, let the magic unfold,
In a palette of laughter, be daring and bold.
For in every splash, there lies a sweet truth,
That life's just a doodle, embrace your own youth!

Arcs of Wonder

A rollercoaster drawing, twirls in the air,
With stick figures screaming, without any care.
An elephant dancing while juggling some pies,
In arcs of pure wonder, imagination lies.

A round cat named Mittens, practicing flips,
While a penguin in boots goes on fun trips.
Sharing pizza parties on treetop high,
With scribbles of joy, let your spirit fly!

In swirls of delight, the silliness blooms,
As balloons float gently from spacious rooms.
What's life but a canvas of curves and of lines?
With laughter like bubbles, your heart intertwines.

So sketch out your dreams, let them take shape,
In arcs and in zigzags, let the giggles escape.
For in every doodle, a world can be spun,
Where fun never ends, and laughter's just begun!

Scribbles of Existence

In margins of pages, I make my stand,
With stick figures waving, a doodle band.
Monsters in my notebook, they dance around,
While life's big questions are lost, yet found.

With wobbly hearts and spirals of time,
Each sketch tells a story, a life in mime.
My cat wears a hat, oh what a sight!
In doodle-land, everything feels right.

A fish rides a bicycle, silly and free,
I scribble my way to infinity.
Lines gushing forth like life's wild stream,
In colors so bright, they make me beam.

So here in my sketches, I'll laugh and roam,
In a world of whimsy, I find my home.
Each scribbled laugh is a chance to play,
In this crazy canvas, I'll forever stay.

The Canvas of Curiosity

On a napkin I draw, as the coffee brews,
Each swirl and squiggle speaks my muse.
A rabbit in a bow tie, a chicken in shoes,
In this quirky gallery, I refuse to lose.

I sketch with abandon, let my mind loose,
An octopus juggling? That's my excuse!
The fridge holds my art, a masterpiece spree,
Every door's a canvas—see what I see!

Wiggly worms and a dancing cake,
A world full of laughter, I happily make.
In every crayon line, joy takes flight,
Curiosity sparkles, oh what a delight!

I'm giggling at doodles, absurd yet sincere,
Unlocking the odd, the peculiar, the sheer.
With each little sketch, the wonder flows,
On this canvas of whimsy, my imagination grows.

Lines of Thought Unraveled

A squiggly line takes a curious turn,
As thoughts start to spiral and twist and burn.
My pen's like a dancer, no plan in sight,
Unraveling musings with sheer delight.

A pie chart of pizza, a graph of fun,
My doodles unite us; we laugh and run.
In corners and edges, my dreams seem to bloom,
Like flowers in spring, they lighten my room.

A sun wearing shades, lounging on a cloud,
In a world of their own, the silly are proud.
My doodles invite in a playful cheer,
In strokes and in colors, I hold them dear.

With moments of madness and giggles, I weave,
A tapestry bursting with dreams to believe.
In lines unconfined, I am set completely free,
Wrapping wisdom in laughter, just doodle and see!

A Quest in Every Curve

In every curl, a riddle hides,
A quest to uncover what laughter confides.
I chart my emotions in wavy schemes,
Lost in the doodles of whimsical dreams.

A dragon in slippers, a knight on a bike,
In this universe, anything can strike!
I scribble to navigate the maze of my mind,
Each curve spins a tale with glee intertwined.

With each playful stroke, I chase down the fun,
A journey in doodles, oh what a run!
From planets of marshmallows to stars made of cheese,
In this land of the silly, I roam with ease.

So here's to the doodles that brighten my day,
In curves and in lines, I'll always play.
An adventure awaits with each little trace,
In the quest to be happy, there's always a space!

Handwritten Revelations

In margins wide, my thoughts collide,
With squiggles here, and circles wide.
A stick figure walks, slips on a dream,
As laughter bursts, it's not what it seems.

Pencil and paper, my quirky booth,
Sketching the world with a wink of truth.
A cat in a hat, a tree in a shoe,
In this silly dance, I find what's true.

With every loop, I laugh and scribble,
Jokes hidden in lines that start to dribble.
What's life but a jest, drawn big and spry?
An artful chaos, oh me, oh my!

So let's embrace this doodle spree,
Where nonsense reigns and minds fly free.
For in each squiggle, a giggle awaits,
A handwritten secret that levitates.

The Artistry of Awareness

Colorful weeds sprout in the lines,
Blobs remind me of odd designs.
A fish in a sweater, an ant on a scene,
What wacky thoughts can doodles glean?

With every stroke, my worries fade,
A unicorn dances, unafraid.
In hindsight, I see, with chuckles galore,
The silly sensations I can't ignore.

Jellybeans tumble on the page,
Each wobbly line, a brand-new stage.
A teapot sings, a cactus twirls,
Life's absurd fun in swirls and swirls.

Through scrawled adventures, I find my flair,
In whimsical worlds, no room for despair.
For in this laughter, creativity flows,
The artistry of joy, everyone knows.

Inked in Elation

A noodle that giggles, a star that winks,
With joyous ink, life's puzzle links.
Frogs in tuxedos, birds in disguise,
Mirth floods my heart, oh how it flies!

Doodles of dreams dance on the page,
My inner clown releases its rage.
With each funny figure, I jive and sway,
Cheesecake giraffes lead the silly parade!

Fanciful thoughts in a convoluted script,
Life's comic relief, wildly equipped.
A world of laughter in shapes and tones,
Where irony sings and sarcasm drones.

So ink out your worries, let whimsy prevail,
Find joy in your doodles, embark on the trail.
With each silly picture, let giggles expand,
Inked in elation, take life by the hand!

Transitory Tales

A doodle's life flickers and spins,
Telling tales of tigers and grinning twins.
With each bold stroke, stories unfold,
In wiggly lines where laughter is gold.

A bubblegum dragon takes flight with glee,
While penguins on roller skates chime in with me.
An elephant wonders, "What's next for me?"
In this whimsical world, we're all fancy-free!

Each sketch tells a story, a twist, a turn,
Where giggles bloom and raucous hearts yearn.
Life's a sketchbook, it's messy and bright,
In this scribble of joy, we take delight.

So grab a crayon, let's color the night,
Transitory tales that thrive on delight.
From whirligig dreams to actual laughs,
In doodle adventures, my spirit drafts!

Threads of Imagination

In corners of my notepad, there lives a cat,
With big ol' eyes and a funny hat.
He chases all my random thoughts,
And rolls around in doodle knots.

A house of cheese, a tree of socks,
My world's a stage for silly clocks.
Each line I draw takes flight and spins,
Where logic fails, the fun begins.

Squiggles turn to dance on air,
A butterfly with polka-dots flair.
With every scribble, truth unfolds,
In colors bright, my heart it holds.

So grab your pen, let chaos reign,
Create a world free from any chain.
For life can be a playful game,
Where doodles grow and thoughts can't tame.

The Art of Wandering Minds

A triangle sings to a wobbly line,
In this strange land, things appear just fine.
A snail wearing shoes talks about his speed,
He pauses to nibble on a chocolate bead.

A fish on a skateboard whirls through the page,
While a tree tells jokes from its leafy stage.
With every squiggle, my brain starts to tease,
And turns mundane worries into a breeze.

A sun with arms gives a warm, tight squeeze,
While doodled clouds scatter giggles with ease.
In this messy art, I drop my fears,
And draw out a world that tickles and cheers.

So let your pencil wander the track,
Where silly and strange are right at your back.
In the dance of your doodles, the joy swells,
And paints life's worries with chuckles and bells.

Breath of the Unwritten

On a blank canvas, my thoughts take flight,
With a dragon shaped like a pickle in sight.
He breathes out rainbows in every direction,
Creating a scene of bizarre perfection.

A moon that giggles and rolls in delight,
Makes shadow puppets that dance in the night.
Each scribbled star jumps with vibrant flair,
Telling stories of wonders found almost anywhere.

Worms in bow ties share their wise views,
About the best snacks on a rainy day blues.
As laughter and doodles collide and entwine,
I realize this chaos feels just divine.

So let's craft the absurd and doodle the strange,
Let colors and shapes continuously change.
In the breath of each doodle, there's laughter and light,
Where life's little oddities take joyful flight.

Doodles of Dawn

With morning light, my pen starts to play,
Sketching odd creatures that brighten the day.
A pancake with legs runs out for a jog,
Chasing a cat that's dressed as a frog.

A sun wearing shades, so cool on the rise,
Winks at a teapot that whistles and flies.
In this hour of joy, my dreams take the stage,
And dance to the tune of a whimsical age.

A pencil parade marches down the lane,
Carrying giggles like balloons on a train.
Each stroke brings laughter, each line brings a grin,
In this swirling world where fun can begin.

So join me in doodles as dawn greets the sky,
In a land made of laughter, let your worries fly.
For in this chaos, we find what is true,
Life's best moments are drawn out by you.

Fragments of a Starlit Dream

In a notebook, I scribble all day,
Squiggles and swirls lead my thoughts astray.
A cat with a hat, a fish with a shoe,
What does it mean? I haven't a clue!

The stars laugh at my doodles, it seems,
As I dive through my chaos of colorful dreams.
An octopus balancing notes on a beam,
Life's just a puzzle, or so it would seem!

Birds in bow ties dance under the rain,
While ants in a band play a tune quite insane.
Each line is a laugh, each curve is a cheer,
Sketching my way through the nonsense I steer!

With crayons in hand, I've a compass of fun,
Navigating nonsense until day is done.
A world made of laughter, uncharted by eyes,
Inviting the viewer to join in the cries!

Whimsical Whorls

A doodle, a giggle, a twist and a turn,
In vibrant hues where my wild thoughts churn.
A fish juggling marbles? Oh, what a sight!
This is the circus of my mind's delight!

Curly-whirly snails in boots made of funk,
Swinging their shells while they happily skunk.
Where dinosaurs ride on a skateboard with flair,
Life isn't boring, it's art in the air!

Mice in disguise doing the tango,
While pie charts are dancing with a flamboyant mango.
Each line a new treasure, each shade a new laugh,
I'm charting my journey through doodles and half!

With whimsy, I weave stories quite bright,
Coloring chaos till it feels just right.
Life's tangled in laughter, with joy in my hand,
In doodles I find a whimsical land.

A Dance of Lines and Shapes

Circles are spinning, triangles sway,
In a dance of confusion, who's leading today?
A square with a tutu, how splendidly weird!
These shapes hold the secrets that I've never feared!

Lines leap and stumble across the page wide,
Tracing the laughter I feel inside.
A rollercoaster ride of curves and delight,
Who knew my scribbles could take flight at night?

Wiggly worms in bowler hats prance,
While polka-dots giggle in a stylish dance.
Every loop turns a frown into glee,
Life's a big circle, come dance it with me!

With my pencil, I sketch out the fun,
In a world of shapes, the laughter's begun.
Navigating through doodles, let's tilt and weep,
This journey of wonder is ours to keep!

Uncharted Territories of Thought

In lands of whimsy, my doodles expand,
With each crooked line, I explore the unplanned.
A rabbit with glasses, a whale in a hat,
Here in my doodle-land, where silliness sat!

Through mazes of colors, I wander and rove,
Chasing strange creatures that frolic and grove.
A chicken on stilts plays a tune with a frog,
In this odd little world, I'm a joyful dog!

Each scribble a journey, each dash a new quest,
In valleys of laughter, I find the best zest.
Juggling chain saws, or maybe just dreams,
This life is a canvas soaked in wild themes!

With my mind as a compass, I map out the fun,
In this crazy expedition, we're never outrun.
Each doodle a story, a laugh-rich delight,
In uncharted territories, we dance through the night!

Hues of Introspection

In crayon hues, I scribble dreams,
Mixing giggles with silent screams.
A stick-figure dance, oh what a sight,
A doodle party in black and white.

With every stroke, a joke unfolds,
Tangled lines tell tales of bolds.
Lost in a maze of whimsical flair,
Life's intricacies, I can scarcely bear.

A cat with wings, a fish that hops,
Sidewalk chalk becomes the backdrop flops.
Under the sun, my paper pal smiles,
Writing nonsense across the miles.

Laughter echoes in the margins wide,
Ink spills secrets I can't abide.
As stickmen run in a silly race,
In this jester's world, I've found my place.

A Cartography of Curves

In the land where doodles sway,
Curvy paths lead me astray.
Maps with squiggles, dotted lines,
A compass points to where the fun shines.

Mountains made of crumpled pages,
Wandering through imaginary stages.
Rivers of ink flow freely here,
Navigating sketches without fear.

Each spiral twist's a brand new quest,
Cartoon monsters put to the test.
I climb the peaks of silly thoughts,
With every dip, joy never rots.

Here laughter's the only sound,
In this artwork, I'm spellbound.
A planet ruled by whims and grooves,
In this chaos, my spirit moves.

Illustrations of Infinity

Endless loops, a loop-de-loop,
Drawing circles with a silly scoop.
The ink runs wild, a cheerful spree,
What's this doodle? It's possibly me!

Infinity laid out in loops,
Where unicorns play with paper scoops.
A flip-flop fish on a skateboard rides,
Through oceans of chaos, my laughter glides.

Thoughts take flight on paper planes,
Written whims wash away all pains.
Every doodle's a new delight,
In this doodle life, everything's alright.

Stick figures argue, a comical scene,
What's the matter? But they're all so keen!
In this gallery of giggles and cheer,
I find my purpose with a scribble near.

Conversations with Paper

My paper talks back with every stroke,
A silent friend, it never goes broke.
Images leap from each inkling made,
Sharing secrets in the shade.

Doodles giggle, wiggle, and sway,
Chatting quietly in their own way.
What wisdom lies in a scribbled note?
As laughter flows in a paper boat.

Each swirl a thought, absurd yet bright,
Characters debate, oh what a sight!
A paper plane soars, it has its say,
In this canvas world, I'm king for a day.

With ink on my fingers, I scribble fast,
In silly conversations, I'm unsurpassed.
A world where ideas frolic and play,
These dialogues with paper? They make my day.

Inkblots of Inner Reflection

On napkins bright, my thoughts collide,
With doodles wild, my dreams can't hide.
A cat with wings, a fish on a bike,
All through my doodling, I take a hike.

In every squiggle, a giggle is found,
Lost in the scribbles, I'm joyfully bound.
A dragon rides a unicorn's tail,
Through silly sketches, I set my sail.

My thoughts take shape in bizarre displays,
With ink and laughter, I spend my days.
A tree that dances, a moon that sings,
Each doodle uncovers the joy it brings.

Through inkblots strange, I find what's true,
In colorful chaos, I'm painted anew.
A world of laughter, so carefree and bright,
In tiny sketches, I find pure delight.

Tangled Threads of Imagination

With crayons bright, my thoughts unwind,
In tangled threads, new worlds I find.
A noodle monster in a chef's hat,
Every silly doodle wears a funny spat.

Between the swirls, a story's implied,
With each little scribble, I take a ride.
A bear that dances on a trampoline,
In wacky dreams, I laugh and glean.

I draw my worries in a blink,
A frowning fish that can't quite swim, I think.
With every line, I find some cheer,
In doodles wild, my thoughts are clear.

From tangled sketches, a giggle will bloom,
In a world of whimsy, there's always room.
A playful heart in a canvas unfurled,
Through laughter and ink, I paint my world.

Charting the Unseen Journey

With pencil in hand, I sketch my fate,
Map of my dreams, let's celebrate!
A rocket powered by a marshmallow,
In my silly world, there's no room for mellow.

Lines twist and turn like a playful stream,
With each silly doodle, I plot my dream.
An octopus chef with pancakes to toss,
Through laughter and ink, I'm never at a loss.

Invisible paths drawn in bright hues,
Each scribble whispers its own fun clues.
A snail in a hurry, with shoes made of crocs,
Dancing through life, in my wacky box.

In this chart of life, I'll always roam,
A paper plane in search of home.
Sailing on giggles, I draw my delight,
With a dash of humor, my canvas is bright.

Scribbled Secrets of the Heart

With every stroke, my secrets come alive,
In doodles that dance, my thoughts contrive.
A heart wearing glasses, trying to read,
In this silly world, I plant my seed.

A fish in a suit, so classy and grand,
Scribbles tell stories no one could have planned.
With laughter and ink, I whisper my dreams,
In every sketch, a joke softly gleams.

In the margins of life, my heart finds a rhyme,
Through artful jests, I dance with time.
A chair that giggles beneath my rear,
In my doodle universe, I shed every fear.

So flip through these pages, my funny parade,
With scribbled secrets, my worries all fade.
In the tapestry of doodles, I find my part,
As humor and joy weave through my heart.

Unfolding Uncertainties

A squiggle here, a swirl there,
Chasing thoughts like a furry hare.
What does this scribble really mean?
Is it a tree or a dancing bean?

Crayons fight for a chance to play,
Colors jostle, come what may.
A maze of lines, so out of hand,
Is that a plan or a soggy sandwich stand?

Each doodle laughs, a giggling friend,
Maybe they know where this will end.
Shrug of the shoulders, let's have some fun,
Life's a sketch, not just a pun!

With highlights bright and shadows deep,
In circles wide, the thoughts will leap.
On this paper, a wild parade,
Make sense of chaos? Let's not be afraid!

Lines that Listen

A wiggly line listens, or so it seems,
Telling secrets born from dreams.
A rectangle nods, it's a wise old soul,
While circles bounce and lose control!

What did I scribble? Who can decipher?
An owl or a cat? A strange new cypher?
With every stroke a giggle does rise,
Artistic mishaps, to everyone's surprise!

Pencil tantrums, eraser fights,
Who rules the world? The paper invites!
Squiggly thoughts pirouette and spin,
In the world of doodles, let the fun begin!

Oh, the magic that colors can share,
A rainbow sigh, a doodle flare.
Lines are listening, silent and sly,
Waiting for giggles or a silly hi!

Emotional Cartoons

A stick figure frowns, but it's all in jest,
With comical tears, it's quite the mess.
A goofy grin takes center stage,
These doodled feelings are all the rage!

A thought bubble pops, what a delight,
Ideas like popcorn, they take flight!
With each funny sketch, laughter ignites,
Cartoons on a quest for uncertain heights!

Doodled dilemmas, oh what a trip,
A paper boat on a watercolor slip.
With whimsy and charm, the pencil glides,
Turning life's woes into comic rides!

Unruly curls and smiley twirls,
The heartbeats dance, their fun unfurls.
Each drawing a tale, absurd and true,
Who knew that sketches could feel so blue?

Traces of the Soul

Scribbles whisper, secrets they keep,
Lines that giggle while we sleep.
A doodle parade, what do they say?
Are they mapping a wild getaway?

With splashes of paint, we let it flow,
Each little mark tells something we know.
From nonsense curls to wild zigzags,
Life's a riddle wrapped in silly flags!

A heart, a star, or a silly face,
In sketches we find our rightful place.
Tracing feelings from funny to deep,
Doodles remind us, in laughter we leap!

With every flick, we search and plan,
To sketch out who we really am.
In the world of doodles, we all take a stroll,
A whimsical journey, traces of the soul!

The Geometry of Emotions

In circles we spin, in lines we draw,
My doodles reveal the quirk of my flaw.
Triangles whisper, squares shout with glee,
Each corner a story, just wait and see.

Octagons laugh at my wobbly curves,
While rectangles tease with their sturdy verbs.
In this tangled web of silly design,
I find that my chaos feels quite divine.

Squiggly strokes trace a jumbled thought,
As laughter erupts from the lines that I've wrought.
The angles of joy, they bounce all around,
In this messy art, my bliss can be found.

Doodles that Define

With a scribble and a squiggle, I sketch out my day,
As my pen starts to dance, all my worries decay.
A cat with three legs, a fish with a hat,
In this quirky gallery, don't worry, don't chat.

Each doodle a clue, like a riddle I seek,
With smiles on the page, I can laugh at the bleak.
A sun that's a cat, and clouds made of cheese,
In this doodle world, my heart finds its ease.

I scribble my dreams with a splash of pure fun,
The absurdities flourish, igniting the sun.
In these wacky designs, what's lost can be found,
With lines that entwine, my thoughts dance around.

Unraveled Mysteries

In a doodle detective's whimsical quest,
I pen silly scenarios, ignore all the rest.
A donut-shaped planet, a squirrel in a cape,
Sketching the oddity, that's my escape.

The mysteries blend in colors so bright,
Where laughter erupts from my art every night.
When thoughts turn to scribbles in unexpected ways,
I unravel the nonsense and cherish the haze.

What if trees could giggle? What if birds wore boots?
In this world full of giggles, my spirit hoots.
Through each stroke of humor, I take a new glance,
To find joy in the doodles, I give life a chance.

Picturing Life's Quandaries

Life's puzzles unfold in a doodly delight,
With ink spills and chuckles, I sketch day and night.
A noodle for dinner, a moon made of cheese,
Doodling absurdity brings me to ease.

What's up with the penguins sitting at the bar?
Drawing each riddle, I say, 'How bizarre!'
With fluffy pink elephants juggling some fruit,
Life's wonders are found in each whimsical root.

Each question a canvas, each answer a line,
With laughter and whimsy, my worries decline.
Picturing life's quirks, I find laughter's true way,
In doodles I treasure, where silliness plays.

Tangles of Thought

In scribbles and squiggles, ideas collide,
A cat with a top hat, enjoying the ride.
Noodle-shaped notions dance and delight,
As I ponder the world in colors so bright.

A donut-shaped planet spins on a string,
While rubber band rainbows begin to take wing.
I chase after thoughts that hop like a frog,
In a world made of doodles, there's never a fog.

Stray doodles of wisdom on napkins abound,
The secrets of life in each sketch can be found.
With wiggly lines weaving tales so absurd,
In the realm of my doodles, no truth goes unheard.

So grab a warm drink and pick up a pen,
In this curious chaos, it all starts again.
With laughter and doodles, we make our own way,
Finding joy in the scribbles that brighten our day.

Etching a Curious Heart

A heart with a mustache, oh what a sight,
Chasing a pickle that glows in the night.
Ideas like confetti are tossed in the air,
Each one a treasure, unique and rare.

My thoughts take a spin on the doodle-shaped wheel,
A dragon with glasses, it's all quite surreal.
In this silly realm where my fantasies play,
Life's questions lead laughter, come join the fray!

With every small doodle, a giggle takes flight,
A fish in a tuxedo feels just so right.
These curious etchings bring joy to my mind,
In laughter, we find what we wish to unbind.

So let's draw our dreams with a splash of delight,
In quirky creations, we soar to new heights.
Through fancies and doodles, my heart's set to roam,
In a whimsical world, I've found my true home!

Paperbound Dreams

In the margins of pages, I draw and I muse,
A snail in a bowtie sings ballads of blues.
With swirls of confusion, I sketch out my fate,
Each doodle a door to the whims I create.

A cupcake on skates glides across my mind,
While fish wearing sneakers are quite hard to find.
Life's canvas is vast, and I doodle with glee,
In my paperbound dreams, I'm forever carefree.

With circles and zigzags, my worries dissolve,
In the land of my doodles, the strange is resolved.
A unicorn prancing through fields of green grass,
With laughter and doodles, I let moments pass.

So let's fill the pages with colors and fun,
In this paperbound journey, the laughter's just begun.
With each little doodle, my spirit ignites,
In this wacky adventure, life's humor delights!

Fleeting Visions

A fish wearing a hat swims in a stream,
While clouds made of candy float by like a dream.
With doodles that twinkle in the light of the sun,
Each sketch is a giggle, a joke on the run.

A pasta-shaped sun, it smiles and it spins,
While raccoons in tuxedos are planning their wins.
Life's bizarre moments unfold with a laugh,
In fleeting visions, I discover my path.

With doodles that dance in the corners of time,
My pen likes to wander, it's simply sublime.
A monkey on roller skates zips through the air,
In this world of my doodles, there's magic to share.

So grab your own paper, let's unleash the fun,
In these fleeting visions, our laughter's just begun.
With whimsical sketching, I'll find my own beat,
In the charm of this doodle, my life feels complete!

Visual Verities

In margins wide, I sketch my thoughts,
A cat in a hat, with shoes and socks.
Where do we go when ideas collide?
To a world of doodles, with laughter as our guide.

A stick figure dances, with grace and flair,
While a donut rolls by, without a care.
In squiggly lines, my humor spills,
Life's a giggle, with twists and thrills.

In every scribble, a story unfolds,
A fish in a bowtie, so bold yet so cold.
With crayons bright, I color my dreams,
Turning nonsense to joy, or so it seems.

So join the parade of a whimsical mind,
Where laughter and doodles are perfectly aligned.
With each little drawing, my spirit takes flight,
In this silly realm, everything feels right.

The Heart's Canvas

With a nodding flower and a grinning sun,
Life's a sketchbook, full of fun.
I doodle my feelings, with laughs and with sighs,
A dragon that giggles, with twinkling eyes.

The raccoon wearing glasses, reading a book,
Finds wisdom in nonsense, come take a look!
Each line I draw fills a void in my chest,
In this playful world, I feel truly blessed.

A quirky parade, with elephants prancing,
In the margins of life, my thoughts keep dancing.
Bubbles of laughter, flying up high,
A poodle in space, oh what a fly!

Every doodle's a heartbeat, a wink, and a cheer,
Life's funny little tidbits, I hold so dear.
In this canvas of joy, I find my own way,
Doodling my heart out, day after day.

Echoes of the Unwritten

In the corners of pages, my sketches take shape,
With monsters in pajamas, escaping fate.
Each scribbled line sings of laughter and cheer,
Chasing shadows of worries, I've tossed in the rear.

A snail in a top hat, so suave and so neat,
Whispers witty secrets while shuffling his feet.
In doodles I wander through wind and through rain,
Finding joy in the madness, and humor in pain.

A parade of doodles, with colors so bold,
In a world where the silly and strange can unfold.
With laughter, I stretch out my imagination,
Unwritten echoes turn into celebration.

So here's to the doodles, my cheerful retreat,
In the chaos of life, they're the rhythm, the beat.
With each tiny picture, a smile I ignite,
In scribbles and giggles, my spirit takes flight.

Doodles Beneath the Surface

In the margins of my page, a cat,
Wearing a hat, what a curious spat!
A fish on a swing, flying so high,
Maybe we're all just fish in disguise.

A rocket ship, chasing a doughnut,
While a snail jogs, just for the fun of it.
What do these sketches try to convey?
Perhaps they're just lost in the fray.

A grumpy old frog playing the lute,
Dancing with clouds, in bright yellow boots.
What goblins and fairies find our delight,
Is it wrong that this makes me feel right?

So I doodle away, with laughter and cheer,
Finding deep meaning, at least I hold dear.
Are these mere scribbles on paper laid down?
Or the secrets of joy, in a whimsical town?

Musings in Margin Spaces

In the corner of notebooks, a puppy does bark,
Chasing its tail, a revolution in the dark.
A cupcake explodes with a rainbow of sprinkles,
Is it utter madness, or the bliss that twinkles?

A dragon with socks, who plays bingo at noon,
Mimicking humans, under a crescent moon.
Each scribbled remark, a question so grand,
"What on earth makes a unicorn stand?"

A taco on a skateboard, oh what a thrill,
Zooming past worries, climbing every hill.
Are these just jests that my mind tries to stack,
Or are they the truths that I never hold back?

So I scrawl in the margins, my mind starts to race,
Finding the meaning in this silly space.
Laughing at nonsense like it's the best rule,
In this doodle-eyed world, I'm the jester-cool.

Ephemeral Etchings

With a wink and a giggle, I draw a green lace,
Connecting two planets in a far-out place.
A sock puppet captain, declaring a war,
On wayward thoughts that flee through the door.

A fish in a tuxedo, sipping sweet tea,
Contemplates life while perched on a tree.
Are these odd visions just making me smile?
Or do they hold wisdom, albeit in style?

The doodles come alive, in ways I can't sense,
A brontosaurus strums a guitar with immense.
Each sketch adds a layer to thoughts in a whirl,
Do they lead to wisdom, or a tangled twirl?

So I pause and I ponder, at these doodles of mirth,
Finding sweet laughter, the truest of worth.
In lines that are silly, and colors so bright,
In these fleeting moments, there's dance and delight.

The Graffiti of the Soul

A scribbled heart, with a smiley face,
Whimsy kicks in, like a vibrant embrace.
Sprinkling joy on a dreary gray wall,
What secrets do these sketches hold, after all?

A penguin in sunglasses, struts with such flair,
While rats in chic coats throw a fashionable air.
Is this the canvas of dreams laid so bare,
Or just wild imaginations, floating in air?

A robot who dances with an old pine tree,
Leaves rustling tales of how life ought to be.
These strokes of delight, each brush of the pen,
Echo laughter and joy, again and again.

So let's scribble freely on paper and minds,
In doodles and sketches, true freedom binds.
With laughter and colors, we craft from our soul,
In this playful wonder, we find our true goal.

Sketches of Existence

In margins bright, I scribble dreams,
With wobbly lines and ice cream themes.
A doodle here, a laugh drawn there,
Life's a sketch, and nothing's rare.

With every stroke, my worries fade,
In stick-figure worlds, I'm unafraid.
A sudden blip, a crooked grin,
Oh, the wonders that I find within.

While rabbits dance in top hats tall,
And fish wear boots, I sketch it all.
Each little whim, a joyful cheer,
In these odd shapes, I feel no fear.

So I draw my path, one curve at a time,
In colors bright, I chase the rhyme.
In every doodle, a spark of cheer,
Life's sweet antics made crystal clear.

Scribbles on the Heart's Canvas

A heart-shaped cat on a skateboard flies,
With curly tails and googly eyes.
I doodle my hopes, my dreams, my snacks,
In silly loops, no time to relax.

Cheese wheels roll in a bright parade,
As I sketch my world, I'm never delayed.
Maybe a donut with arms to dance,
In this doodle life, I take every chance.

Each scribble tells a tale so grand,
Of flying pizzas and a marching band.
I laugh aloud, my worries flee,
In every line, there's joy for free.

So grab your pen, let's join the fun,
Let's doodle beneath the shining sun.
With colors that pop and silly beats,
In this vibrant world, life's a treat.

Lines and Laughter in the Margins

In the corner of my notebook, a fish wears a hat,
He tells me stories, all jiggly and flat.
With every line, I feel it clear,
Life's best moments draw laughter near.

Stick-figure friends in a silly race,
Running with giggles, all over the place.
They tumble and crash, but never frown,
In this doodle chaos, we wear the crown.

An octopus playing a drum set loud,
While a peanut dances, oh so proud.
These little sketches bring joy anew,
In every dot, there's a laugh or two.

So let the margins be wild and free,
Where every line is a jubilee.
Life's a big doodle, come play along,
With laughter and whimsy, we can't go wrong.

The Art of Unwritten Stories

A couch that sings, oh what a sight,
With polka dots glowing, it shines so bright.
In each funny sketch, a tale unfolds,
Of wild adventures and treasures untold.

A bird in a tie, strutting with flair,
On a pogo stick, it jumps through the air.
I chuckle and giggle at every line,
In this zany world, everything's fine.

The aliens laugh as they land on my page,
With crayon spaceships, they dance and engage.
Each doodle a wonder, a pure delight,
In these crazy sketches, everything's right.

So put down your worries, just grab a pen,
Let's dive into doodle-land, again and again.
With laughter and joy, let's create our tale,
In this whimsical journey, we will not fail.

The Palette of Possibility

With crayons bright and moods to sway,
I scribble nonsense every day.
A chicken wears a crown, oh dear,
Is it a joke or a life career?

In doodles deep, I find my cheer,
A monster's grin, a tiny deer.
Each stroke unveils a silly tale,
Where laughing clouds begin to sail.

A sun that dances, a moon in glee,
Stick figures playing hide-and-seek, you see.
In laughter's grip, I catch a glimpse,
Of all the colors life can skimp.

So here I stand with art so bold,
In crayon land where thoughts unfold.
With every mark, I take a flight,
Embracing joy in doodles bright.

Cartography of Inward Exploration

On paper maps of smiley faces,
I trace my thoughts through silly places.
A treasure chest of giggles found,
In doodled paths where joys abound.

I wander through a rainbow town,
Where ice cream monsters spin around.
My compass points to marshmallow land,
With jellybean trees all nicely planned.

Not all who doodle are lost at sea,
Some sail on boats of fantasy.
Each line I draw reveals the jest,
Of life's sweet riddle, just a quest.

So grab your pens and let's embark,
In joyful lines, we'll leave a mark.
With laughter near and worries far,
We'll find our joy in every star.

Shapes of Serenity

In circle dreams and triangle smiles,
I find my peace in doodled miles.
A square that spins, a heart that sings,
In this odd world, joy simply clings.

Ellipse of giggles, the world so round,
Where laughter loops and twirls abound.
A zigzag path of silly strife,
Leads me closer to the zest of life.

A wobbly star tips from the moon,
While jellyfish dance to a quirky tune.
In every squiggle, calm abounds,
Where happiness in colored shapes is found.

So let's embrace this silly art,
With every scribble, we won't depart.
Within these shapes, my thoughts take flight,
In doodly peace, everything feels right.

Freehand Revelations

With pens in hand, my thoughts take flight,
In random scribbles, wrong feels right.
I draw the cat that bakes a pie,
While frogs in hats sing lullabies.

A hand that waves from summer skies,
And clouds that tickle with their size.
A fish on roller skates glides by,
In doodled worlds, I laugh and sigh.

Each squiggle brings a new surprise,
Where silly faces meet the wise.
In every doodle, truths collide,
Revealing joy I cannot hide.

So let's embrace this jolly spree,
In doodles wild, we're truly free.
With every line, more fun unfolds,
In this freehand life, let laughter mold.

The Art of the Unknown

In the margins of my page, they roam,
Little squiggles that feel like home.
A dragon here, a cat in socks,
My life's chaos in silly blocks.

With every curve, my thoughts expand,
Each doodle a moment, just like sand.
They dance and twirl, a crafty show,
Whispering secrets I hardly know.

Oh, what wisdom in a circle wide,
Maybe my heart wants to be a tide?
Or perhaps a fish in a funky hat,
Living my dreams, imagine that!

So I scribble on, with laughter loud,
In this doodle realm, I feel so proud.
A masterpiece made of silly fright,
In the art of unknown, I find delight.

Scribbles of Self

A wiggly line represents my stride,
Scribbles of me, with nothing to hide.
I draw my fears, my joy, and glee,
A spaghetti of thoughts, wild and free.

In yellow suns and greenish moons,
I splash my life to funny tunes.
What's this? A toaster with legs on the run?
I guess my mind loves to have some fun!

Shapes that bounce like a rubber ball,
A doodle that echoes my inner call.
Each line I trace, a part of my quest,
In the scribbles of self, I feel so blessed.

A crooked smile and a jiggly grin,
In these lines, I find my kin.
A world of oddities, rib-tickling charm,
In the art of silliness, I stay warm.

Inkling Journeys

With every stroke, a journey begins,
Where fairies wear hats and laugh like twins.
My ink spills tales of the bizarre,
A fish that dreams of being a star.

A sidewalk sprinting beneath my pen,
Round and round, where's it going? When?
Each inkling leads to a new delight,
A doodle world bursting bright!

Curved lines that giggle, and zigzag cheer,
In my notebook's chaos, I'm the pioneer.
A monster munching on socks, how absurd!
Each drawing's a flight, a wild word.

So let's scribble our way on this page,
With giggles and twists of an artist's rage.
In the inkling journeys, we break the norm,
With laughter as fuel, our stories warm.

Drawn Connections

Two dots and a line, oh what have I found?
A connection so silly, yet profound!
A brain with arms, doing the cha-cha,
While my pencil dreams of a quirky gala.

A noodle that sings and a shoe that flies,
Each drawing unveils a surprise in disguise.
Laughter binds the shapes I create,
Bringing joy, it's never too late!

With every loop, a friend appears,
In the funny shapes, I conquer my fears.
A rainbow that giggles and dances around,
In drawn connections, a friendship is found.

So grab your pen, let's doodle the night,
Fill the pages with laughs, oh what a sight!
For in these sketches, our spirits rise,
Finding connections, we'll claim the skies.

The Language of Lines

In a world of squiggles, we start to see,
Curvy connections that set our minds free.
Each circle's a giggle, a line is a grin,
In the ink of our madness, let the laughter begin.

Crayon conspiracies, colors collide,
The scribbling secrets we can't seem to hide.
With each playful doodle, a story unfolds,
In the margins of life, adventures retold.

Wiggly wonderlands paint the mundane,
With a wink from the page, we're never quite sane.
Life's a cartoon, with punchlines and twists,
In the humor of sketches, reality's missed.

So pick up a pencil, let your thoughts roam,
In the doodle dimensions, you're always at home.
Each artful absurdity, a chuckle in time,
In the language of lines, find your own rhyme.

Beyond the Scribble: A Voyage

Set sail on a napkin, a doodler's delight,
With waves of dark ink in the glow of moonlight.
Drawn tiny adventures, each one a treasure,
The doodles we make bring untold pleasure.

Erasers are anchors that keep us in check,
While zigzags and swirls take us over the deck.
Pirate ships made from paper and dreams,
In the vast ocean of scribbles, nothing's as it seems.

With margins as shores, we sketch 'til we tire,
Sailing through thoughts, setting hearts afire.
Each swirl is a wind, blowing free through the sky,
In this cruise of the mind, we never say die.

So grab a pen high and let laughter steer,
For the best kind of voyage is with friends who are near.
Through each goofy doodle, let's chart our own fate,
In this ship of imagination, we'll never be late.

The Artistry of Everyday Questions

What does a doodle of breakfast imply?
Is it art or a cue for a pancake supply?
Each stroke holds a riddle, a laugh in disguise,
In the halls of our minds, curiosity flies.

Why do squiggly lines seem to flutter and dance?
Are they leading us somewhere or stuck in a trance?
Each doodle's a riddle, a puzzle to crack,
In the coloring book of life, there's never a lack.

Can a doodle bring answers? Oh, the joy of the quest!
Like finding a sock that was lost with the rest.
As we scratch our heads, laughter comes to light,
In the doodles we ponder, there's always delight.

With crayons for wisdom, and sketches for grace,
Life's questions seem smaller in this colorful space.
So doodle away, let your thoughts play their part,
For the artistry of queries is a doodler's true art.

Picturing the Unanswerable

In the realm of doodles, the questions just buzz,
What's the meaning of life? Turns out, it's a fuzz.
With stick figures debating in circles so wide,
Finding answers in nonsense, our laughter our guide.

Why is the sky blue, and where goes the sun?
Each doodled distraction, all in good fun.
With squiggles as answers and scribbles as truth,
We paint our confusion, embracing our youth.

A stick-man philosopher with wild, crazy hair,
Gives lectures on doodles, with nibbles to share.
In this gallery of giggles, philosophy struts,
With nonsensical wisdom, collectively nuts.

So let's raise our pencils and sketch out the unknown,
In the bizarre doodle world, we're never alone.
For the unanswerable questions get laughter, not sighs,
In the pictures we draw, the absurdity flies!

www.ingramcontent.com/pod-product-compliance
Lightning Source LLC
Chambersburg PA
CBHW051654160426
43209CB00004B/897